I ♥ Craft

SEWING

Rita Storey

W

FRANKLIN WATTS

LONDON • SYDNEY

First published in 2014 by
Franklin Watts
338 Euston Road
London NW1 3BH

Franklin Watts Australia
Level 17/207 Kent Street
Sydney NSW 2000

Series editor: Sarah Peutrill

Packaged for Franklin Watts by Storeybooks
rita@storeybooks.co.uk
Designer: Rita Storey
Editor: Sarah Ridley
Crafts made by: Rita Storey
Photography: Tudor Photography, Banbury
www.tudorphotography.co.uk

A CIP catalogue record for this book is available
from the British Library.

Printed in China

Dewey classification: 646.2

ISBN (hardback): 978 1 4451 3080 4
ISBN (library ebook): 978 1 4451 3081 1

Cover images: Tudor Photography, Banbury

Franklin Watts is a division of Hachette Children's Books,
an Hachette UK company
www.hachette.co.uk

Before you start

All of the projects in this book require a sewing needle, sewing
pins and scissors; some require glue. When using these things we
would recommend that children are supervised by a responsible
adult. Always return sewing needles and pins to a safe place,
such as a needle case or a pin cushion.

Please note: keep homemade toys and products
away from babies and small children.
They cannot be tested for safety.

Contents

Needle and Pin Case

This cute dog is guarding a secret. Open his mouth to discover a spiky surprise.

You will need:

* thin white paper and pencil
* pink felt, 17cm x 7cm
* black felt, 2 x 8cm x 4cm, 1 x 3cm x 3cm
* cream felt, 8cm x 5cm
* brown felt, 19cm x 9cm
* sewing pins
* needle with a big eye
* scissors
* embroidery thread
* fabric glue
* 2 buttons

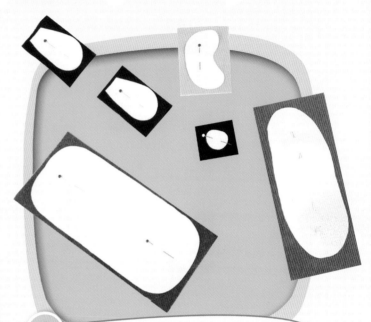

1 Trace the templates on page 31 onto thin white paper. Cut out the shapes. Pin the shapes onto the felt pieces as shown in the picture above.

2 Cut around the templates. Take out the pins and remove the templates.

Put the needles and pins you use to make the crafts in this book inside this handy case for safe-keeping.

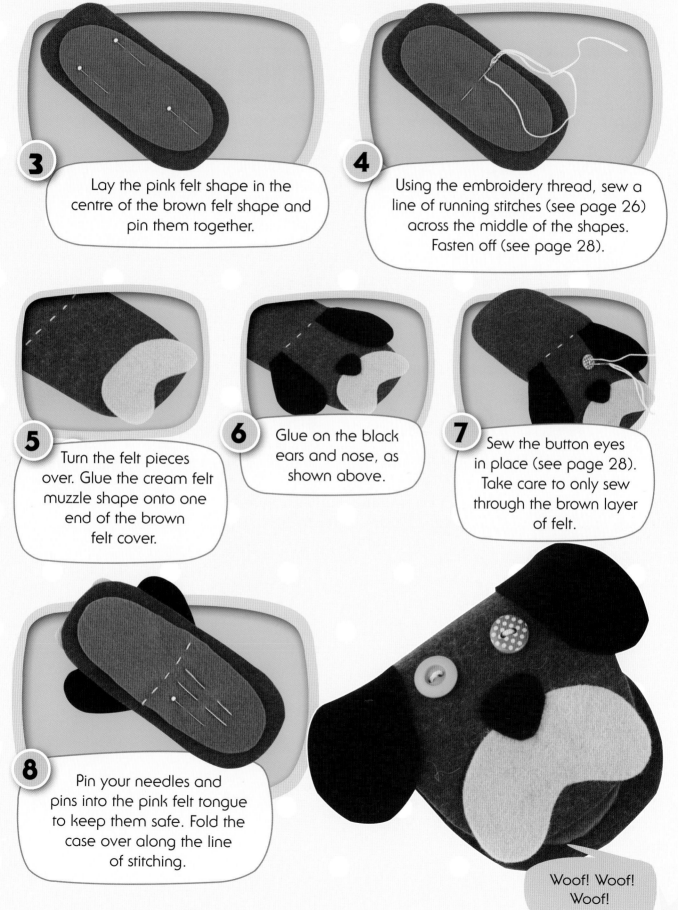

3 Lay the pink felt shape in the centre of the brown felt shape and pin them together.

4 Using the embroidery thread, sew a line of running stitches (see page 26) across the middle of the shapes. Fasten off (see page 28).

5 Turn the felt pieces over. Glue the cream felt muzzle shape onto one end of the brown felt cover.

6 Glue on the black ears and nose, as shown above.

7 Sew the button eyes in place (see page 28). Take care to only sew through the brown layer of felt.

8 Pin your needles and pins into the pink felt tongue to keep them safe. Fold the case over along the line of stitching.

Woof! Woof! Woof!

Tissue Holder

A small packet of tissues can be turned into a pretty gift with the help of some felt and a few simple sewing stitches.

You will need:

* a small packet of pocket tissues
* piece of orange felt, 15cm x 13cm
* bottle cap or coin, 3cm in diameter
* pen
* sewing pins
* scissors
* fabric glue
* embroidery thread
* needle with a big eye
* green felt
* a craft jewel

1 Place the bottle cap or coin in the corner of the orange felt. Draw half way around the bottle cap or coin to create a pen mark along the shortest side of the felt.

2 Move the cap or coin along the edge of the felt and draw around it again and again, as shown, to create a scalloped pattern.

3 Use scissors to cut along your pen line.

4 Place half the tissues on top of the felt, in the centre, as shown.

5 Fold the bottom edge up over the tissues. Fold the scalloped edge down to overlap the straight edge. Pin in place on both sides to form a pocket.

6 Using the embroidery thread, sew along one side with running stitch (see page 26). Fasten off (see page 28). Repeat on the other side. Remove the pins.

7 Cut a small heart shape from the green felt, using the template on page 31. Glue it onto the top flap as shown.

8 Glue a craft jewel onto the centre of the felt heart.

When the tissues are finished it is easy to refill the holder with some more.

Teddy Bear

This adorable bear is made from fleecy fabric. Can you resist a cuddle?

You will need:

* sewing pins
* thin white paper and pencil
* blue fleece fabric,
  1 x 44cm x 26cm,
  1 x 10cm x 10cm
* scissors
* needle with a big eye
* embroidery thread
* toy stuffing from a craft shop
* small black button
* 2 teddy-bear eyes
* ribbon

Create a different cuddly animal by drawing the outline as a template, and following the steps on this page.

1 Trace the template on page 31 onto folded thin white paper and cut it out. Unfold the template. Fold the larger piece of fabric in half and pin the template to it.

2 Cut out around the template shape. Take out the pins and remove the template. Now you have two fabric bear shapes.

3 Trace the muzzle template on page 29 onto thin white paper and cut it out. Pin it onto the fabric. Cut out around the shape. Take out the pins and remove the template. Sew running stitches (see page 26) all around the outside of the felt circle.

4 Gently pull the thread so that the stitches gather together to form a fabric bag. Do not pull tight.

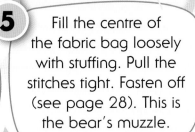

5 Fill the centre of the fabric bag loosely with stuffing. Pull the stitches tight. Fasten off (see page 28). This is the bear's muzzle.

6 Lay the muzzle, gathered side down, onto the head of one bear shape. Sew five small running stitches right through the muzzle and the bear shape to make the mouth, as shown. Fasten off.

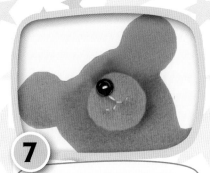

7 Sew on a button (see page 28), just above the mouth.

8 Push the pin attached to one of the teddy-bear eyes through the fabric above the muzzle as shown. Clip on the back part. Repeat with the other eye.

9 Place the two shapes one on top of the other, with the face on the outside. Match the edges. Pin them in place.

10 Use running stitch to sew around the edge. Leave a 3cm gap on the side of one leg. Fill the bear with stuffing. Sew up the last 3cm using running stitch. Fasten off. Tie the ribbon around the bear's neck.

Hug me!

Plastic Bag Jellyfish

All sorts of different fabrics can be sewn, including plastic!

You will need:

* black bin liner
* scissors
* china plate, 28 cm in diameter
* 2 colourful plastic bags
* needle with a big eye
* embroidery thread
* glue

1 Place the plate on the black bin liner. Cut around it (you do not need to be very accurate).

2 Sew large running stitches (see page 26) all the way around, 1.5cm from the edge. Pull the needle clear of the thread.

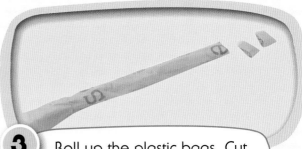

3 Roll up the plastic bags. Cut across the rolled up bags.

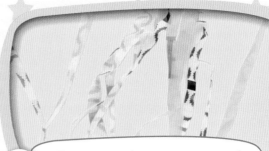

4 Open out the cut pieces of plastic bag to make long strips of plastic.

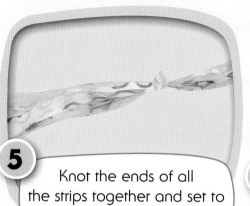

5 Knot the ends of all the strips together and set to one side to use in step 7.

6 Return to the circle of black plastic (step 2). Pull the stitches to gather them up. Stuff the black plastic jellyfish body with the rest of the plastic bags and the bin liner.

7 Push the knotted end of the plastic strips into the jellyfish body.

8 Thread the needle again. Pull the stitches tight. Fasten off (see page 28).

9 Cut out two bigger circles from the coloured plastic bags and two smaller ones from the bin bag, as shown. Glue on as eyes.

Run around outside with your jellyfish to make the tentacles wave about.

Hanging Hearts

These pretty hearts would look good hanging on a Christmas tree. Or you could thread them onto a string and hang them above a picture or a mirror.

To make one green and blue heart you will need:

* thin white paper and pencil
* scissors
* blue fabric, 7cm x 10cm
* green fabric, 15cm x 9cm
* sewing pins
* needle with a big eye
* embroidery thread
* toy stuffing from a craft shop
* 16cm length of ribbon

1 Trace the large heart template on page 29 onto thin white paper. Cut out the shape. Fold the green fabric in half. Pin the shape onto the fabric. Cut around the shape and take out the pins. Remove the template.

2 Trace the small heart template on page 29 onto thin white paper. Cut out the shape. Pin the shape onto the blue fabric. Cut around the shape and take out the pins. Remove the template.

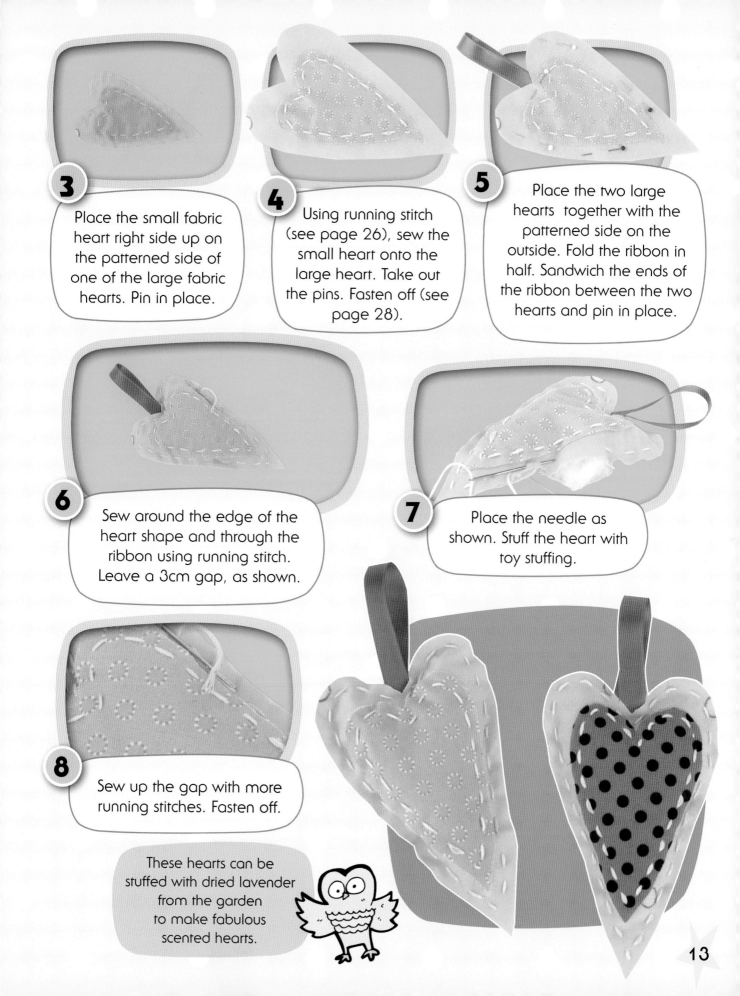

3 Place the small fabric heart right side up on the patterned side of one of the large fabric hearts. Pin in place.

4 Using running stitch (see page 26), sew the small heart onto the large heart. Take out the pins. Fasten off (see page 28).

5 Place the two large hearts together with the patterned side on the outside. Fold the ribbon in half. Sandwich the ends of the ribbon between the two hearts and pin in place.

6 Sew around the edge of the heart shape and through the ribbon using running stitch. Leave a 3cm gap, as shown.

7 Place the needle as shown. Stuff the heart with toy stuffing.

8 Sew up the gap with more running stitches. Fasten off.

These hearts can be stuffed with dried lavender from the garden to make fabulous scented hearts.

Yo-yo Necklace

Fabric jewellery is often in fashion. Make this stunning fabric necklace and wait for the compliments!

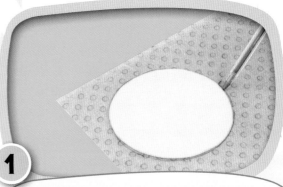

You will need:

* sewing pins
* scissors
* thin white paper and pencil
* pink polka dot fabric, 10cm x 10cm
* yellow polka dot fabric, 10cm x 20cm
* green polka dot fabric, 10cm x 20cm
* needle with a big eye
* embroidery thread
* 3 orange spotted buttons
* 2 yellow spotted buttons
* 50cm length of 1cm wide orange ribbon

1 To make the pink polka dot fabric yo-yo, trace the large circle on page 29 onto thin white paper and cut it out.
Place the circle onto the pink polka dot fabric. Draw around the shape. Remove the template.

2 Sew running stitches (see page 26) all around the outside of the circle, 5mm from the edge.

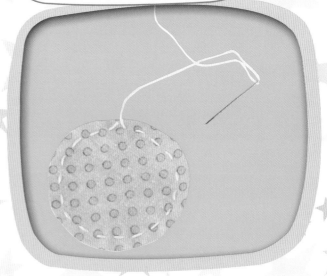

3 Pull up the stitches tightly to make a small fabric bag. Fasten off (see page 28).

4 Flatten the bag so that the gathers are at the top.

5 Sew on a spotted yellow button (see page 28) right through the fabric layers. The button will cover the raw edges of the gather.

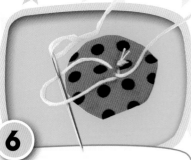

6 Fasten off the stitches at the back.

7 Follow steps 2 – 7 to make four more fabric yo-yos. Make a small and a large green polka dot yo-yo and the same in yellow polka dot fabric.

8 Place two fabric yo-yos together with the buttons facing out. Oversew (see page 27) to join them together with three stitches. Fasten off the thread. Repeat this step to join all the yo-yos to each other, as shown in the photo below.

9 Cut the ribbon in half. Stitch the end of one piece of ribbon to the back of a small fabric yo-yo, as shown. Repeat on the other side. To fix the necklace around your neck, tie the ribbons in a bow.

Use scraps of old fabric to make another totally unique vintage necklace.

Flower Cushion

This stylish cushion would be great for your favourite soft toy or you can make a bigger version for your bed. If you don't like orange, choose a colour to suit your room.

To make the orange cushion you will need:

* ⋆ 2 x squares of orange felt, 20cm x 20cm
* ⋆ thin white paper and pencil
* ⋆ sewing pins
* ⋆ scissors
* ⋆ needle with a big eye
* ⋆ embroidery thread
* ⋆ toy stuffing from a craft shop
* ⋆ large button

1 Trace the flower template on page 30 onto thin white paper. Cut it out. Place the orange felt squares on top of each other, matching up the edges. Pin the template onto the orange felt.

2 Cut out around the template. Take out the pins and remove the template. Pin the felt flowers together.

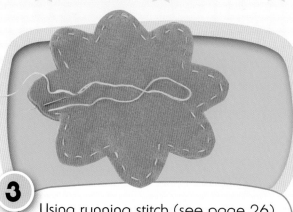

3 Using running stitch (see page 26), sew a line of stitches 1cm in from the edge. Leave a gap of 3cm, as shown. Take out the pins and the needle.

4 Stuff the shape with toy stuffing.

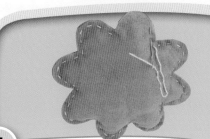

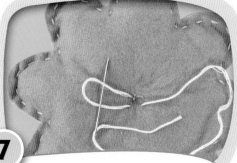

5 Sew up the gap you left in step 3. Fasten off (see page 28).

6 To sew on the button, take a new piece of thread with a knot in the end. Push the needle right through the centre of the felt cushion. On the other side, thread the needle through one hole in the button and back down through the other hole. Repeat.

7 To finish, push the needle right back through the cushion to the side without the button. Pull tight. Fasten off.

If you want to make a bigger cushion, use two felt squares 60cm x 60cm.

Glove Monster

Turn an old glove into a pet monster. Or you could turn a pair of gloves into matching monsters for you and a friend.

You will need:

* a glove
* embroidery thread
* needle with a big eye
* sewing pins * scissors
* thin white paper and pencil
* red felt, 6cm x 4cm
* pink felt, 7cm x 5cm
* toy stuffing from a craft shop
* 2 googly eyes
* fabric glue

Ask permission before you cut up a glove to make this monster.

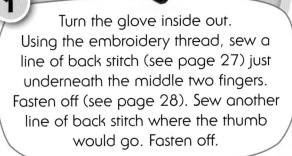

1 Turn the glove inside out. Using the embroidery thread, sew a line of back stitch (see page 27) just underneath the middle two fingers. Fasten off (see page 28). Sew another line of back stitch where the thumb would go. Fasten off.

2 Cut off the glove fingers and thumb 1cm above the line of stitches to leave just the first and fourth fingers of the glove. Keep the fingers for step 7. Turn the glove the right way out.

3 Trace the templates on page 29 using thin white paper. Pin the mouth template to the red felt and the teeth template to the pink felt. Cut them out and remove the pins.

4 Stuff the fingers and the body of the glove with toy stuffing.

5 Using embroidery thread, sew big running stitches (see page 26) around the bottom of the glove.

6 Pull the thread carefully until it is tight. Fasten off.

7 Take one of the glove fingers you cut off in step 2. Stuff it with toy stuffing. Sew running stitches around the opening. Pull the stitches tight. Fasten off.

8 Sew the gathered glove finger onto the stuffed glove to form an arm using oversew stitches (see page 27).

9 Repeat steps 7 and 8 with the other glove finger to create a second arm. Attach it to the opposite side of the glove.

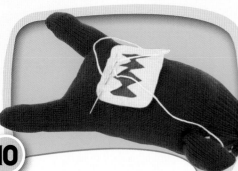

10 Put the pink felt teeth on top of the red felt mouth. Pin in place. Using running stitch, sew them onto the glove monster. Remove the pins.

11 Glue a googly eye onto the top of each finger.

Aaaaghhh!

Felt Cookie

These felt cookie toys look good enough to eat! They are great fun to make as well.

To make the chocolate cookie you will need:

* thin white paper and pencil
* sewing pins * scissors
* needle with a big eye
* square of dark brown felt, 8cm x 8cm
* square of dark pink felt, 8cm x 8cm
* green, white, dark brown and pink embroidery thread
* toy stuffing from a craft shop

For the white iced cookie you will need all of the above and:
* square of white felt, 8cm x 8cm
* square of light brown felt, 8cm x 8cm

1 Trace the cookie templates on page 29 onto thin white paper. Cut them out.

2 Pin the cookie shape onto the dark brown felt. Cut it out.

3 Remove the pin. Repeat to make a second felt cookie shape.

20

4 Pin the icing template onto the dark pink felt. Cut it out. Remove the pin and template.

5 Use the green embroidery thread to make small straight stitches on the pink felt, as shown. Do the same with the white embroidery thread.

6 Using small running stitches (see page 26) and the pink thread, sew the felt icing shape onto one of the felt cookie shapes. Fasten off (see page 28).

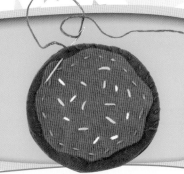

7 Place the two brown felt cookie shapes together. Use dark brown thread to oversew (see page 27) around the outer edge to join them together. Leave a gap of about 2cm. Keep the thread still attached to the needle but pin the needle carefully to the pink felt icing.

8 Put some toy stuffing inside the felt cookie. Oversew the gap. Fasten off.

9 To make the second cookie, repeat steps 2 – 8 using light brown felt, white felt and white, pink and green embroidery thread.

Superstar Shoe Bag

Turn an old T-shirt into a shoe bag fit for a superstar.

You will need:

* old T-shirt
* scissors
* sewing pins * embroidery thread
* needle with a big eye
* safety pin
* 1m length of ribbon
* thin white paper and pencil
* yellow felt, 15cm x 15cm
* green felt, 10cm x 10cm
* blue felt, 5cm x 5cm

Ask permission before you cut up a T-shirt to make this shoe bag. Which pair of shoes will you keep in the finished bag?

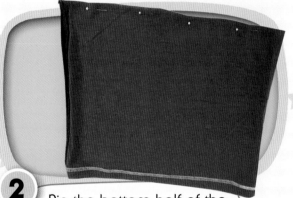

1 Lay the T-shirt on a flat surface. Cut across the T-shirt just under the arms.

2 Pin the bottom half of the shirt together, as shown.

3 Use back stitch (see page 27) to sew across the pinned edge. Fasten off (see page 28) and remove the pins.

4 Using a pin, unpick 1cm of the hem of what was the bottom of the T-shirt. Attach a safety pin to the end of the ribbon.

5 Ask an adult to help you feed the safety pin and ribbon through the hem and out through the hole again.

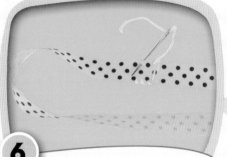

6 Place the ends of the ribbon together. Oversew (see page 27) the ends together, by oversewing along the edges for 1cm, as shown.

7 Trace the star templates on page 32. Cut them out. Pin the medium-sized paper star on the green felt and cut it out.

8 Repeat step 7 to cut out: one big yellow felt star, one medium-sized blue felt star and two small felt stars (yellow and green).

9 Sew the small stars onto the bag using cross stitch (see page 28). Sew the other stars onto the bag using running stitch (see page 26).

Undersea Mobile

Transport yourself under the sea with this fishy mobile.

For the mobile you will need:

* thin white paper and pencil
* sewing pins
* glue and spreader * scissors
* embroidery thread
* needle with a big eye
* glitter glue
* toy stuffing from a craft shop
* goggly eyes (two for each fish)

For the spotted fish, you will need:

* orange or purple felt,
  2 x 13cm x 8cm
* scraps of purple and yellow felt
  (for the spots)

For the striped fish you will need:

* yellow felt, 2 x 13cm x 8cm
* scraps of purple blue and orange
  felt (for the stripes)

For the seaweed you will need:

* 2 x squares of green felt,
  19cm x 19cm

1 Trace the fish template on page 30 onto thin white paper. Cut it out. Place the two orange felt squares on top of each other, matching up the edges. Pin the template onto the orange felt. Cut out the fish shape. Take out the pins and remove the template.

2 Cut out small circles from the felt scraps to decorate the felt fish. Glue them onto the fish.

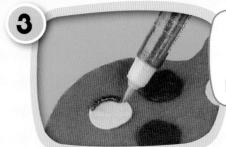

3 Outline the circles with glitter glue. Leave to dry.

4

Place the two felt fish shapes on top of each other. Oversew (see page 27) to join the fish together. Leave a 3cm gap on the tail, as shown.

5

Stuff the fish with toy stuffing. Sew up the gap. Fasten off (see page 28).

6

Glue a googly eye on each side of the fish. Repeat steps 1 – 7 to make a purple spotted fish.

7

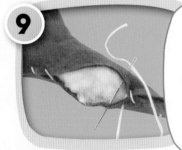

To make a striped fish follow steps 1 – 7 but cut out stripes from the felt scraps instead of spots.

8

Trace the seaweed template on page 30 onto thin white paper. Cut it out. Pin the shape onto the green felt and cut it out. Repeat to make a second seaweed shape.

9

Oversew around the edge of the seaweed shapes to join them together. Leave a 3cm gap. Stuff the seaweed with a small amount of toy stuffing. Oversew the gap to finish and fasten off.

10

Thread a needle, tie a knot at the other end and use it to sew a fish to the seaweed, as shown. Fasten off and repeat to join the other fish to the seaweed. Hang up your mobile in your bedroom.

Sewing Stitches

Before you start

1 Slide one end of the thread through the eye in the needle.

2 To make a knot in your thread, form a loop. Pass the needle through the loop and pull tight.

Running stitch

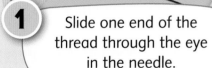

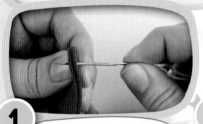

1 Push the needle through the fabric from the back.

2 Pull the needle and thread through to the knot.

3 Push the needle back through the fabric about 5mm away from where the thread came through.

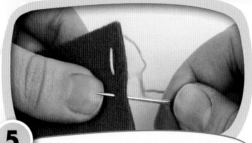

4 Pull the thread through the fabric until it is tight, but not too tight.

5 Push the needle through from the back about 5mm away from the first stitch. Pull the needle and thread through and repeat along the length of the fabric.

6 Running stitch can be used to join two pieces of fabric or as decoration.

Oversew

1 Push the needle through the fabric from the back.

2 Pull the needle through to the knot. Pass the needle around the edge of the fabric and push the needle through the fabric from the back, a bit further along.

3 Repeat to make more stitches.

Back stitch

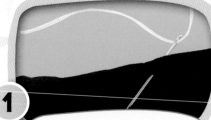

1 Push the needle through the fabric from the back. Pull the needle and thread through to the knot.

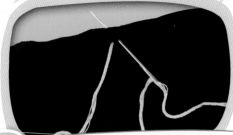

2 Push the needle back through the fabric about 5mm to the right of where the thread came through. Pull the thread through the fabric until it is tight, but not too tight.

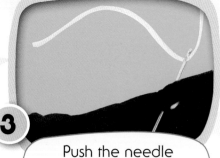

3 Push the needle through from the back about 5mm to the left of the first stitch. Pull the needle and thread through.

4 Push the needle back through the fabric alongside the first stitch.

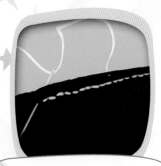

5 Repeat steps 3 – 4 along the length of the fabric.

27

Cross stitch

1 Push the needle through the fabric from the back. Pull the needle and thread through to the knot. Push the needle down through the fabric where you want the stitch to end.

2 Push the needle up from the back between the two stitches and to the left of them.

3 Push the needle back through the fabric on the other side of the stitch, as shown above, to make a cross.

Sewing on a button

1 Push the needle through from the back of the fabric and through one of the holes in the button. Pull the thread through to the knot.

2 Push the needle back down through the second hole. Pull the thread through to the end. Repeat and fasten off.

Fastening off

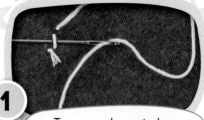

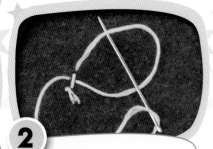

1 To stop the stitches coming undone, slide the needle under one of the stitches at the back of the fabric.

2 Pull the thread through so that you make a loop.

3 Pass the needle through the loop and pull it tight.

Templates

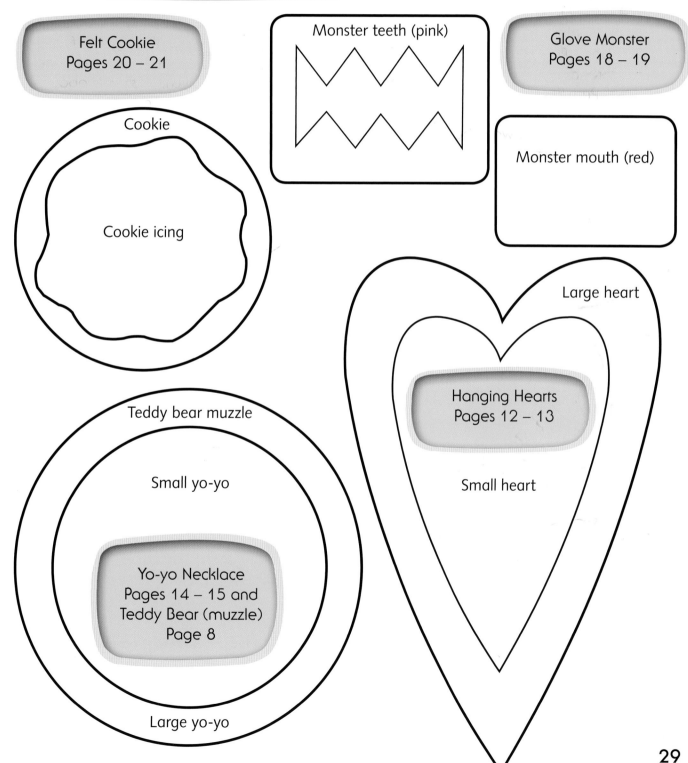

Felt Cookie
Pages 20 – 21

Monster teeth (pink)

Glove Monster
Pages 18 – 19

Cookie

Cookie icing

Monster mouth (red)

Large heart

Hanging Hearts
Pages 12 – 13

Teddy bear muzzle

Small yo-yo

Small heart

Yo-yo Necklace
Pages 14 – 15 and
Teddy Bear (muzzle)
Page 8

Large yo-yo

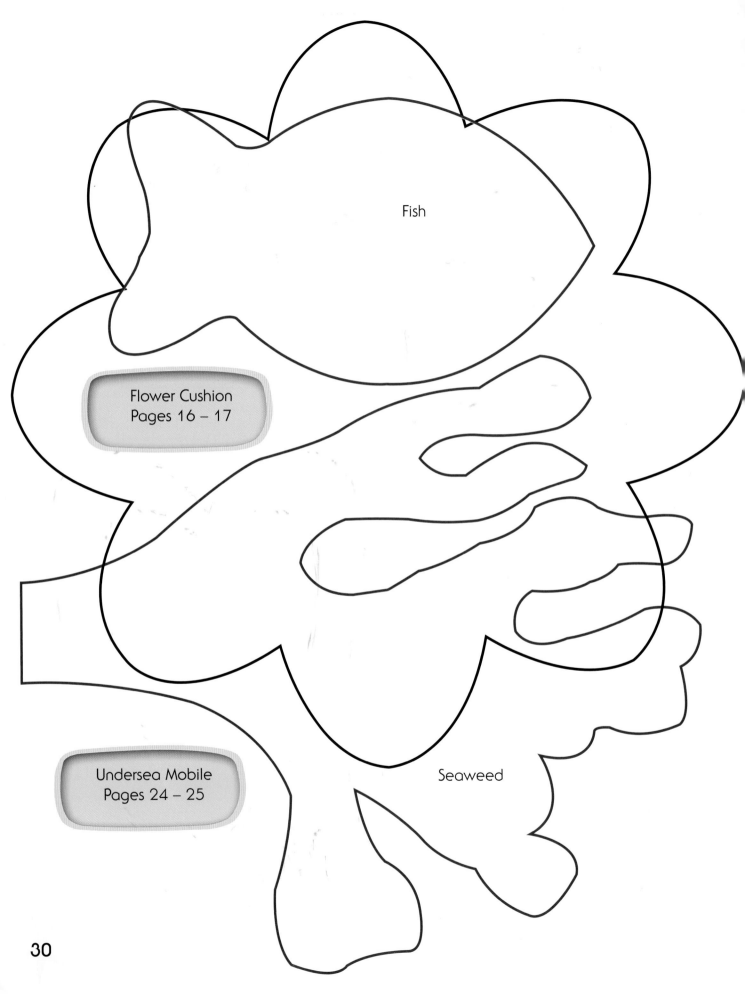

Fish

Flower Cushion
Pages 16 – 17

Undersea Mobile
Pages 24 – 25

Seaweed

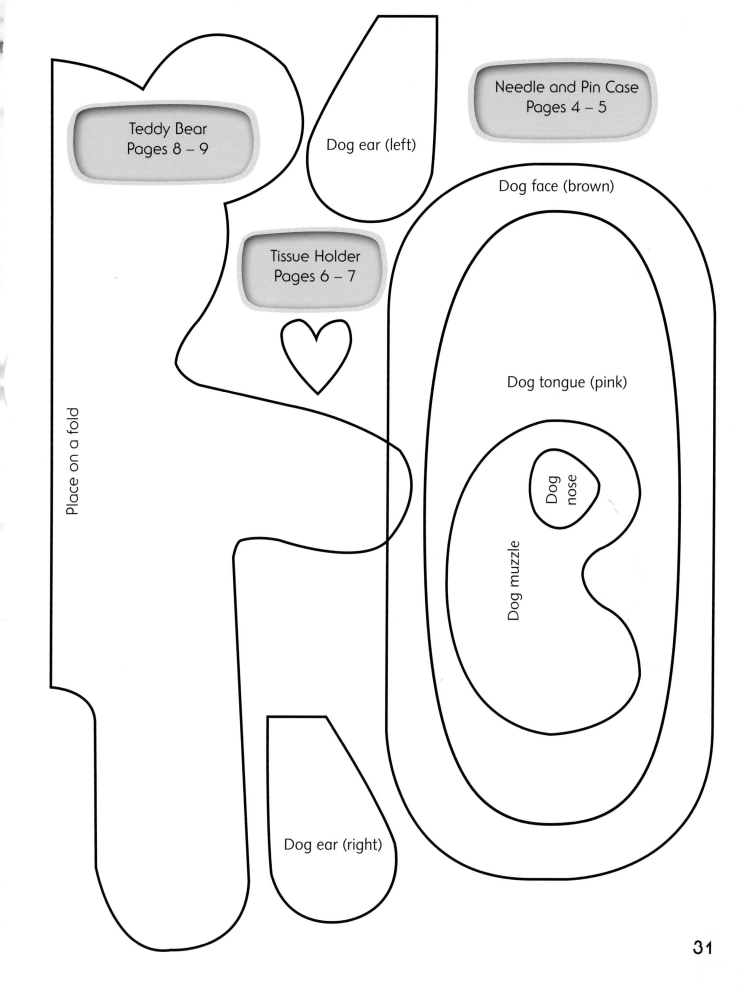

Teddy Bear
Pages 8 – 9

Dog ear (left)

Needle and Pin Case
Pages 4 – 5

Dog face (brown)

Tissue Holder
Pages 6 – 7

Dog tongue (pink)

Dog nose

Dog muzzle

Place on a fold

Dog ear (right)

31

Superstar Shoe Bag
Pages 22 – 23

Large star

Medium star

Small star

Index

Further Information

Websites
For short videos that demonstrate basic sewing stitches, go to:
www.charlieandhannah.co.uk/sewing-videos

Books
'The Complete Book of Sewing' by Chris Jeffreys (Dorling Kindersley, 2006)
This book covers all the techniques and tips you need for sewing projects.